I See You.
Do You See Me?

A young reader's introduction to bird watching

PAM SHEPPARD

LifeRich Publishing is a registered trademark of The Reader's Digest Association, Inc.

LifeRich Publishing books may be ordered through booksellers or by contacting:

LifeRich Publishing
1663 Liberty Drive
Bloomington, IN 47403
www.liferichpublishing.com
1 (844) 686-9607

ISBN: 978-1-4897-2762-6 (sc)
ISBN: 978-1-4897-2764-0 (hc)
ISBN: 978-1-4897-2763-3 (e)

Print information available on the last page.

LifeRich Publishing rev. date: 10/22/2020

Hello, young readers!
I love to watch birds. They
fill me with delight.
I find them in grasses, trees,
or lakes, or high in flight.
Each bird is amazing
and one of a kind.
I'd like you to meet them, though
they may be hard to find.
Let's go an adventure, a
game of hide-and-seek.
Look through your hand binoculars,
turn the page, and have a peek.
Your friend,
Grandma Pam

P.S. If you look closely, you can
also spot a ladybug, a frog, and a
butterfly on each hide-and-seek page.
Good luck, my little adventurers!

Cardinal

Female
Duller colors

Male
Brighter colors

I'm a musical red cardinal with black on my face.
My female stays with me at our nesting place.
We don't mind the winter, and we even hop on snow.
So grab some yummy birdseed and throw, throw, throw!

American goldfinch

Male
Brighter colors

Female
Duller colors

I'm a yellow goldfinch with wings white and black.
My strong little beak gives seeds a whack, crack, crack!
"Po-ta-to-chip, po-ta-to-chip," I sing and I cheep.
I turn grayish brown when winter is bleak.

Goldfinches are small birds, and that helps them balance on small twigs. They only weigh as much as five quarters. Have you ever seen a goldfinch jump from twig to twig?

Ruby-throated hummingbird

Male
Brighter colors

Female
Duller colors

I'm a ruby-throated hummingbird, green and bright.
I move forward and backward, left and right.
My wings flap so fast; you can hear them if you try.
I hum-zizi-hum as I fly through the sky.

I see you. Do you see me? Find six of us to play hide-and-seek.

Hummingbirds are tiny and fast. Their wings beat fifty to two hundred flaps per second. Their females lay eggs the size of peas.

Barred owl

Male
Smaller

Female
Larger

I'm a barred owl with big dark eyes.
With silent wings I hunt through the skies.
I'm the only owl that hoots night and day.
"Who cooks for you? Who cooks for you?" you can
hear me say.

I see you. Do you see me? Find seven of us to play hide-and-seek.

When courting, the male and female barred owls bob their heads back and forth, raise their wings, and sing together. It is pretty spooky to hear, especially at night.

Mute swan

Male
Similar appearance

Female
Similar appearance

I'm a mute swan with a slender neck of white.
Admirers say I am a lovely sight.
Baby swans are *cygnets*; we protect them all the day.
They climb on our backs when they're just too tired to play.

I see you. Do you see me? Find twelve of us to play hide-and-seek.

The word *mute* means "unable to speak." Mute swans do not get their name because they are silent, but because they are not as noisy as their loud, honking cousins.

American coot

Male
Similar appearance

Female
Similar appearance

I'm an American coot, gray from head to foot.

I dive in the water to eat tasty plants and roots.

I'm definitely not a duck, for their webbed feet just aren't right

For running on the water before splish, splash, flight!

I see you. Do you see me? Find thirteen of us to play hide-and-seek.

American coots lay their eggs in floating nests that they build on top of the water. Don't worry; they don't float away.

Turkey vulture

Female
Similar appearance

Male
Similar appearance

I'm a turkey vulture with red skin on my head.
High in the sky I smell animals that are dead.
My vulture cleanup crew keeps the world from smelling stinky.
So shout "Thank you!" to our friendly crew who cleans your road by eating.

Bald eagle

Female
Larger

Male
Smaller

I'm a bald eagle, and my head and tail are white.
My long, wide wings help me soar through my flight.
I swoop to the water, sharp talons on my feet,
To capture swimming fish for my little ones to eat.

I see you. Do you see me? Find six of us to play hide-and-seek.

Bald eagles have large nests that they make in big trees. Every year they add more to their nests. These nests can weigh as much as a small car. Did you know that the bald eagle is the national emblem for the United States? It symbolizes freedom.

Mallard duck

Female
Duller

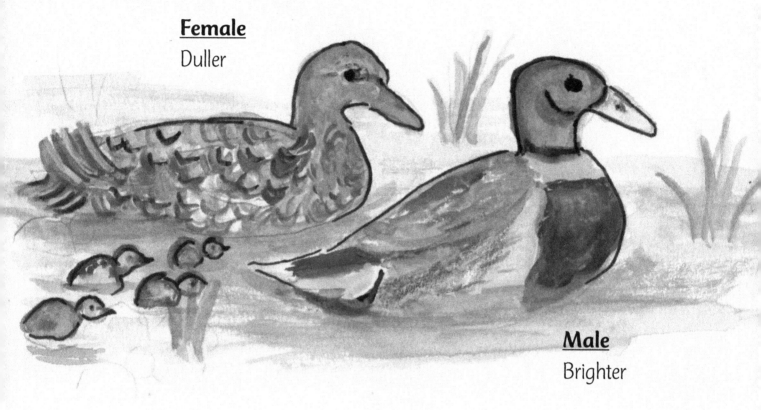

Male
Brighter

I'm a mallard duck with green head and yellow beak.
You can find me swimming on a lake or in a creek.
We males hiss and hiss, and our females say, "Quack, quack."
We tip underwater as we look for tasty snacks.

Mallard ducks lose their flying feathers twice a year and can't fly for a few weeks!

Eastern bluebird

Male
Brighter

Female
Duller

I'm a lovely eastern bluebird, and I'm famous for my song.
Can you say "chur-chur-lee"? I sing that all day long.
I eat insects, seeds, and berries, and I love to splish and splash.
Look for me in your backyard or in a birdhouse or a birdbath.

I see you. Do you see me? Find sixteen of us to play hide-and-seek.

About forty years ago new birds came into the bluebirds' territory. The new birds moved into the bluebirds' warm homes and kicked them out into the cold winter. It wasn't long before bluebirds became an endangered species. People like "Mr. Birdman," Al Larson, made many bird boxes as homes for them to stay safe and warm during the cold winters. Now they are no longer endangered.

Downy woodpecker

Male
Red head

Female
White head

I'm a downy woodpecker—black, white, and red.
With my beak I drill holes in trees overhead.
"Tappity-tap, tappity-tap," my head and beak will drum
To find the insects—what a treat! Yum, yum, yum!

I see you. Do you see me? Find twelve of us to play hide-and-seek.

Downy woodpeckers do not sing vocally. Instead, they make rhythmic songs by drumming on pieces of wood and tree bark. Have you ever heard their drumming?

American robin

Female
Duller

Male
Brighter

I'm an American robin, and I'm first to sing at dawn.
We mommies and daddies sweetly feed our young.
I see worms by tilting my head to the side.
Then I gobble them up, and down they slide.

American robin babies are born tiny and helpless. In only two weeks they grow to be the same size as their parents! They stay in the nest for two to three more weeks while their father feeds them and their mother starts a new nest of eggs.

You found us all; now one more game. Point to us when you hear our name.

Cardinal	Mute swan	Mallard duck
American goldfinch	American coot	Eastern bluebird
Ruby-throated hummingbird	Turkey Vulture	Downy wookpecker
Barrel owl	Bald eagle	American robin

You found my feathered friends,
although they hid from you
In grasses, trees, lakes, and sky—
you've learned what they can do.
Keep playing our game of hide-
and-seek, for everywhere in sight
Are birds that sing, birds
that dance, and birds that
fill us with delight.

Your friend,
Grandma Pam

CPSIA information can be obtained
at www.ICGtesting.com
Printed in the USA
LVHW070519201220
674639LV00020B/704